Afowereets Owgun

A collection of dialect words, language and pastimes of a Staffordshire Moorlands village

Afowereets Owgun

Wey didner esk to learn thee neem
An this is ower forever lasting sheem
Funt in a box with all our kin
Ar wish thee cust tell mey weetheest bin

Afowereets Owgun

A collection of dialect words, language and pastimes of a
Staffordshire Moorlands village

Peter Turner

Published by Success Factor Ltd 2017

Copyright © 2016 by Peter Turner

All rights reserved. This book or any portion thereof may not be reproduced or used in any manner whatsoever without the express written permission of the publisher except for the use of brief quotations in a book review or scholarly journal.

First Printing: 2017

ISBN 978-1-326-89026-1

Success Factor Ltd
Glenhough
Sandy Lane
Brown Edge
Staffordshire Moorlands

Orders for the book may be made at:-
www.brownedge.com

Dedication

To the people, past and present, who define the character of this Moorlands village of Brown Edge. Related by blood, marriage and the bond of growing up, working & drinking together.

This is a book about us all.

Contents

Costner Shutner Wutner 1

The A's 3

Brine Edge or Wom 7

The B's 9

Pastimes 13

The C's 15

Confusion 19

The D's & E's 21

Pleen Iteseed 23

The F's 27

Poaching 29

The G's 31

Feytin 33

The J & K's 35

The Mines 37

The L & M's 41

The Skow 43

The N & O's 47

Soolin and Geyzin 48

The P's 57

Keytin 59

The Q & R's 61

Of Pubs and Churches 63

The S's 67

Old Soldiers 69

The T's 71

Dogs & Pigeons 73

The Rest 75

Famous Sons (or daughters) 77

Afowereets Owgun

Acknowledgements

I am indebted to the late Mr John Levitt who, as Director of Adult Education at Keele University, inspired people like myself to value the diversity and origins of the English Language.

Until I met him some 30 years ago now, I had been brought up believing that the way we spoke (our twang), was something to be ashamed of, and of less value than the Queen's English. I remember relaying this to him on our first adult class, his reaction was sheer enlightenment to me.

"The North Staffs dialect is the closest to the original English of any dialect and you will come to see that the dialect most people speak is just the dialect of the home counties" "There is no Queen's English and there is no one who dictates to us how we speak, or indeed what and how we write. English is a spoken and ever changing language"

It was then that I decided to record any interesting anecdotes and dialect words that defined us better and more emphatically as Staffordshire Moorlanders than any mark on a map.

I am also grateful for the permission given to me by the estate of Arthur Berry to quote a section of "The Three and Sevenpence Halfpenny Man" by Arthur Berry, and also the family of William Trebilcock who assisted me to understand how an evangelical Cornishman ended up in our church yard.

Finally I must acknowledge and thank the work my daughter Victoria, undertook to give it a sanity check, a punctuation check, and making it slightly more readable. I know the way I speak is not always grammatically correct! That's the point of the book!

Preface

I have a dilemma! When writing dialect how should I do it? To start with, there is the broad dialect of my youth, the kind of stuff spoken even now in pubs here in the village, and again there are the local variants. Indeed these variants enabled you to identify when people were from further north (Lake), further west (Ched), further south (Potherbs), or further east (Kidcrew). If you take a look on a map you can probably work out where these places are. However *Utcheeter* and *Oositer* are unlikely to be found (Uttoxeter and Wolstanton).

Even the title gave me a few challenges. Should it be *afoweraytes* or *afowereets*? *An dust know, ardunner. It cud bey eether or ayther dependent ow they feylst ar rekon.*

So another issue is that words seem to be jumbled up, or at least follow on with no break. *Anyroodup arv dunneet lark thee seest eet..* This in itself is confusing because when you are *seein* it in Brown Edge, you are using your mouth not your eyes! So *sayin* is seeing and *seein* is saying!

Anyway, bear with me and perhaps you can appreciate the challenges teachers must have had when they tried to teach Brown Edge children what they considered, to be the "correct" way of speaking.

This book is not just about dialect but tries to capture the way in which a community worked, a different way of life than is present today. When you look back even in the last 20 years, communities all over the UK have changed more than we could imagine, Brown Edge is just one of them.

To assist readers all dialect words are in italics.

Afowereets Owgun

Costner Shutner Wutner

Narthen aadoow

That's how two Brownedgers greet each other, perhaps nowadays it's just shortened to *aadoow*. I don't see why we shouldn't start this book off in the same way. So....

Narthen aadoow siree, owat, atorate?

I was brought up in a family business where it was perfectly normal for someone to say, *"Thee costne let that gooite withite gittineet weshed ite".* We had a bus company, one of many similar private operators who used to take workers into the local towns from the villages that surround Leek and the Potteries. The garage where they were based was my home.

The garage seemed to attract characters, and people would walk in and have a chat. I first noticed a peculiarity of language in general, as there are degrees of North Staffs dialect and the extent to which you spoke it depended upon who you were talking to. If they were also speakers of dialect then the depth of the language unconsciously changed. If Fred or Dan Durber came in and spoke to my Uncle Gordon, then sometimes my dad, who was the youngest of the family, would just laugh at me, and shake his head because the dialect became incomprehensible.

So the first words I learnt were usually based around the workings of the garage, for example we had *lekking* cans and *tundishes* for filling with *watter or waiter* (which is the same thing but changes to fit in with the words around it). The norm was to have sentences made up to include *shutner, costner, wutner, shonner, thee* and *thou*. For example, *"Thee costne goo dine theer sirree, theytl git bowtered up an meyn awee".* We didn't play with marbles they were *shotties, tors or stonnies*, and fireworks were *bunters*.

Now here is my first challenge in writing this book, just how much will people understand of this? This is difficult, as very often we don't know when we are using a dialect word or not. People have often had to occasionally point it out to me, whilst doing a talk or presentation. "Just who is this nesh you are talking about?" Translating words is also difficult because sometimes there is no equivalent. How would you describe *sneeped* (which is the posh version of *sneyped*), in one word?

A bit of digging about the word *sneeped* and it comes from snape an old English word for the poor land around the village. That is, for example the wet marshy area which is ideal for the Snipe, a bird (*brid*) to be found in those areas. So to be *sneeped* describes how you would feel if you were given this poor land to live off by the village chief. I suppose the Snape family would *bey reet sneyped!* And they probably were, as this in all likelihood is how they originally over 1000 years ago, received their name.

In fact, I was *rate snayped* one day when working in Jakarta, Indonesia, training all the Hyundai National Service Managers, when one guy from Syria asked if my Russian colleague could translate into English for them! My accent isn't that broad is it? I felt obliged to explain that I was talking real English not American, but I would slow down so they could appreciate the true English Language.

It can all be a bit confusing so let's start as we did at school with a few words that begin with A.

A bit of a warning here however, when you hear the word *"a"* spoken, it usually means he, and *he* means hay! *"Hey sowd hee ow dee"*. Mmm,…. see what I mean, confusing! How on earth could you tell that he was selling hay all of the day?

The A's

Abide	Stick with or endure	Old English *abidan*
	Abide With Me is sung at many church services, but it is rarely heard in normal or general conversation, Locally, it is often used in the following way, *"Dust noo, ar conna abide im, eys owees got summat mower than theyt".*	
About	Pronounced *Abite*. It doesn't mean "around here" i.e. Are there any mushrooms about. But to get started as in:-	
	"Theytad better get abite it, as itl never be done else".	
Afterings	The last milk from a cow. I have not heard this since I was a child.	
Aftermath	Second crop of grass	Old English
	In the Moorlands the second crop of grass is very important, especially on higher ground. Sometimes weather conditions mean that only one crop of hay is achieved. Therefore in this context, an aftermath is positive but the generally accepted meaning (non dialect) has changed to be negative. i.e. the aftermath of a battle.	*math* mowing
Agate	Busy or going again	Norse *gata*
	Agate is usually used after someone has been ill *"Theytl sown bee agate agin, ite an abite thee costne beyt it"*	
Aired	Warmed slightly	

Afowereets Owgun

	Whilst this word is used quite widely in the UK, as in airing cupboard, it is used exclusively and at the exclusion of tepid. Which is a word I had never heard of until I ventured to Newcastle (under Lyme)	
All but	Nearly	
	"Ar wuz owbut theer n ar funtite ard lefit yonder".	
	"Eh wuz eelin soo much ey wuz owbut jyed"	
Amperlash	Impudence	
	What a great word this is!	
	"Nar dunner giv mey any amperlash yowth. Theetl bey smeylin on tother seydan thee feece"	
And then	Used often at the end of a sentence for no reason! "Nar dunner giv mey any amperlash yowth an then".	
Angry	When a spot or pimple, becomes inflamed the *bleb* turns angry and gathered.	
Apaces	Break up "Ar didner touch it. it just fell apaces"	
Ardoo or (more formally) Adoo	It's not what a couple say when they get married it's the greeting two Brown Edgers say to each other in a morning.	
	"Ardoo sirrey atorate tdee".	
Ark	Sounds like something that should float but it's where you keep corn	
As good as	Nearly	

	It's as good as hafe an hours wowk t theere	
Arns	Wages	Medieval English Ernes
Essgrid and ess hole	It's not just about ashes it's really the bottom of a chimney flue	
Aside	Next to "They cust sit aside mey"	
Asker	Newt	
Averous	Averacious	French averus

Many houses on Brown Edge were built by Harold Bourne. This was one of his lorries parked up years after it did its last trip, outside Bosley Wood Treatment works.

Afowereets Owgun

Brine Edge or Wom

Nowadays the village of Brown Edge stands on the edge of the Staffordshire Moorlands overlooking Cheshire, and what was the industrial powerhouse of our area, Stoke on Trent. It hadn't used to be quite so much of a border village. Stoke on Trent expanded rapidly in terms of output in its main industries; coal, steel and pottery It also expanded in size, taking over Moorland villages such as Norton Le Moors, Milton & Smallthorne. Our village, part of Norton Parish, was not included in this expansion, and so our Moorlands identity has been retained and further expansion resisted.

Looking back, the character of our community has changed significantly, not so much in how it looks but in how people lived their lives. Until the 1980's, men mostly worked down our local pits and the women worked in the Silk Mills of Leek. Boys and girls went to the village school together, and then went to work together. In the evening the men went to the pub. In our village that used to have around eight hundred souls, we had six pubs and a Working Mans Club! If men didn't go out to the pub they were "hen pecked"!

This poem by Mr Reginald Twemlow our Village Policeman (remember them?) sums up village life where people not only worked hard, but also played hard.

The Ode to a Pub

At close of day when toil is done,

They wend their way at setting sun,

Where rural joys still reign supreme,

And form a part of the village scene.

Where tales are told and laughter brings,

The salve that makes the sad heart sing,

And all join in with merry mirth,

Afowereets Owgun

And cares fly out, for them no berth.

The ale that bred fair Englands brood,
Awakes the muse of bardic mood,
And he with songs will loud acclaim,
the joys of love 'twixt maid and swain.

The night wears on and words wax warm,
And some will treat and some will squarm,
But all will hark to the knowing one,
who talks the night till words are gone.

As the hour to part draws sadly nigh,
And tankards filled are now drained dry,
The merry swain calls for another,
And the stranger now becomes a brother.

Then all will sing a roundelay,
And fix a time for another day,
Then sally forth content and full,
Their long goodnights the heartstrings pull.

Oh! let these rural joys remain,
That rid the labouring hearts of pain,
And find such happyness within,
The house they call the "Roebuck Inn".

The B's

Back-end	Autumn. I hadn't even heard of autumn until I went to school, and I still think that back end describes the period from autumn to winter much better than anything else.	
Backstan	Where you bake bread. Well you don't really nowadays but this is the piece of the range or hearth where bread was baked. A bit like a pizza oven!	Old English Bac stan
Badging Hook	Sickle that is used when the oats or barley can't be scythed because it has fallen over	
Bad	To be ill "Ar felt reet bad tdee".	
Bagging	Take food to work	
Bags	To claim "Bags I goo fost"	
Bait	Food you eat outside	Norse beita
Banksman	Foreman	
Bat	To run or move fast "Eys battin on. Ey neyds bey cearful else eyl be catchin isell up".	
Bartered-up	Splashed with mud	
Bass	Poor coal "Arl tell thee if that cool man brings any mower o that bass, arl slat it at im next tarm. Thee costne beyt that olly leen cool"	

Afowereets Owgun

Baum	Plastered	
Beck	Peak of a cap	Medieval English bec
Bedfast	Bed ridden	
Beestings	First milk from a newly calved cow. Prized for its health giving properties. What is strange is that there is always more than one ie pleural	
Bellock	Cow bloating	
Belong	It's strange but people belong to a place or property in our village. *"Hey belongs dine Judfeylt"* as if this was his rightful place! *"Thee cust get back to wear theyt belung ...dine yen"!* (Yen is what we call Endon)	
Belter	Something big and probably good as well. Not sure how/or if that applies to the female form but *"Theyt lucky, ers a belter"!*	
Bing	Trough in front of cows	Norse bingr
Blart	A child crying like a calf does after its mother *"What at blartin at".*	OE blaten
Blaitch	Slap or hit	ME blenchen
Blather	Talking nonsense	Me blather

Bleb	Pimple	
Bloat	A cow mooing excessively	
Bobbing off	Playing truant	ME boben
Bodge	To proke a hole	
Boffle	A chimney boffles back	
Bonny clapper	Sour milk	
Bonk	Hill or house "Thee cust get thesell off the bonk" Means to get out of my house but there are other bonks, a pit bonk, a pot bonk or a skew bonk, and up bonk or dine bonk. Plenty of bonks on Brine Edge	
Borsened	Could mean bored (fed up) or full of food (fed up)	
Brunt	Burned or is it burnt? *"Ays brunt eet ageen"*	
Bread an Cheys	The tip of a young hawthorne stem when sucked or chewed by someone	
Bull-nogger	Millers thumb (type of fish)	
Butty	A member of a work gang	

Afowereets Owgun

Pastimes

When the men were not in the pub, then they had some other favorite pastime. Gardening was an important activity and everyone seemed to have a greenhouse with a stove, so that tomatoes and the other favorite, chrysanthemums could be forced early. There was, of course, two principal reasons for this, feeding your family and the annual produce show, where an intense sense of competition was the order of the day or rather the week before.

I remember on old miner who lived opposite me *Frankie Owdcruft* (Holdcroft) trying to teach me how to grow prizewinning crisses as they were called. For the tightest incurved blooms you had to pot up and compress the soil around the edges really tight. As he told me this it was if he was giving me the keys to the crown jewels. He grew leeks in a drainpipe and his secret weapon was sut. *"It conner bey fresh. Theets gotter av it rotted, covered up so grubs get in it."*

Soot was the one word that didn't follow the normal dialect rules which dictated that a book, a rook, a stook, all sounded like the brown owl, a definite ooo oooo. A cup, a bus, to strut and love were all ʊ sounds defining us as northerners. The south staffs accent has a book sounding like a buk etc. Here though soot was always pronounced sut exactly the same as sit was pronounced which was confusing if you had, like me as a child, sat exactly where the chimbley sweep had deposited his sut! *"Ast sut in t'sut"*

After the weekend of the produce show, the goods were auctioned off for charity. There was many an argument when a slightly worse for wear gentleman returned home with produce that has cost him a small fortune. The cucumber and pair of onions always created a raucus laugh and merriment as they were held aloft by the auctioneer. One of the women would always snigger and pass comments like *"Nar then dunner get thesell any funny ideas our Jack"*

Afowereets Owgun

Even worse was the end of evening sale of chrysanthemums so that the by now drunk men fought to take home to their wives the best displays of flowers at ridiculous prices, thinking that all would be forgiven.

Part of village life were the trips or outings. The club trip was the big one, we didn't have enough buses and had to utilise the services of Procters and Stoniers buses. The picture above would likely be the club trip. Left to right are Arthur Morris, Manny Slater, Alfie Morgan, Tommy Jones Edwin Turner, unknown "Slasher" Challinor & Unknown. Notice the boot open. This wasn't for luggage on these occasions but crates of beer! They were drinking on the way, and on the way back.

The C's

Cack	Excrement or doing something the wrong way *cack handed*	Me cakkin
Cade	Weak lamb or sometimes a child	
Cag-mag	Poor meat	
Cale	Beat or get ahead I have not heard this being used for quite a while but it would be used in this context. *He towd mey as ey would beyt mey but ar caled im.* I wonder if there is any relationship with another expression to get kaylied?	Latin *canto*
Cant	Tell tales. At school there was *"Nowt woss than a cant"*.	
Casey	Leather football	
Carry on	To carry on implies some sort of infidelity	
	"Dust eyer er was carrin on ow tarm an ey never sow it".	
Chincough	I think it's whooping cough but used when parents are warning children to wrap up in winter. *"Git the ganzee on or else thytl catch chincough an then theytl bey there"*. Just where there is, no one knows!	
Chommers	Teeth	
Chops	Mouth	

15

Afowereets Owgun

Chonnock	Turnip	
Chunner	Grumble "Wot at chunnerin at"	
Clem	To be hungry "Arm clemmed deeth sirry" (Starving means to be cold)	
Clog again	To get going again another lease of life	
Clogging on	To reach an old age. "Dust ere ey must bey clogging on a payce"	
Clout	Piece of cloth or clothing. "Cast not a clout till the Mee be ite"	Old English clout
Coat or cote	We don't have pig sty or chicken coup we have pig cotes, pigeon cotes & hen cotes	Old English Cot
Cob or cobbed off	Sweat or angry/agitated "Eys got a cob on an sheys cobbed off abite it, an ow becuz ey was sweatin cobbs an wunner tak eys shirt off".	
Cobbed-up	Cluttered up with rubbish "Ar conner stand beyn cobbed up. Everythin as its pleece and a pleece fer owe".	
Cockstride	Short distance	
Cod	Joke with or to pull someone's leg	

Codge	Patch up poorly *"Theyst meed a rate codge theer"*	
Coffer	Grain storage	Medieval English coefre
Collywesson	Awkward Contrary *"Theyt just lark ar Pel they at, collywessun"*	
Craft	Small field near farm could also be called a fold	
Crog-on	Cheating especially with games involving numbers	
Craft	*"Theyt croggin on. Deck it, if thee dustne theytl av a gobfull of teyth"*.	
Crossomical	Irritating or perverse	
Cunnyfogle	Deceitful	
Cuther	Get heads together for a chat *"Eh up theere cutherin up, must be summat up!*	

Confusion

Another linguistic challenge I had as a lad was understanding that when "outsiders" used the word starving, they really meant *clemmed*. We used starving as meaning we were cold.

"It's starveeshun tedee siree, theytl beter thesell if thee ad a cooton. Arr a pot a lobby wudner goo amiss as arm clemmed deeth".

A couple of other peculiarities. People seem to constantly say *overtook* instead of "overtaken" i.e. *"Weywe overtook bee a car onth rood"*, The use of an h or *aich* in front of a vowel instead of using an, (*"I ate a horange"* instead of 'I ate an orange".) was also challenging, especially when I went to Grammar school to be heducated.

I undertook some research on this strange use of H and found that in fact until the 16th century the use of the letter h in this situation was the norm. Somehow the world passed us by!

Confusion occurred with outsiders (*strugs*) as well, because our village of 800 people, (now expanded to 2000) seemed to primarily consist of a handful of surnames. Mountford, Bourne, Holdcroft, Hargreaves, Goodwin, Simcock, Turner, Dawson, & Pointons. These names were hardly ever used in reality however unless they were used in conjunction with nicknames. Fizza, Workbag, Spot, Pell, Sour, Maunch Razza and so on. Sometimes these names ran in families where you would use the first name as well like Jimmy Cud and Billy Cud. Bar Berrisford, Pup Berrisford or Sap Berrisford. Nicknames sometime morphed, one character was called Worm which has now become Grub.

These names were used consistently and enthusiastically by everyone and signified you were mates. I once committed a faux pas when I addressed Mr Simcock by his nickname, *Bacca.* I didn't know it was his nickname, I thought *Bacca* was his real name. He wasn't too upset, just said I wasn't old enough to call him *Bacca* as his name was Joe Simcock.

Our village lost 28 men in the First War and 16 in the Second. Families lost all the breadwinners, so being a Conscientious Objector was not popular. Indeed they were given the nickname of

Conchie and used to their face by their mates. Our former local District Councilor, confessed to me that she as a child addressed someone as Mr Conchie without realising it was a nickname and a dreadful slur on them.

This isn't the only confusion regarding names for outsiders. Another habit of our village is that girls retain their maiden name. my wife was Janet Scott before she married me, my sister is Janet Turner so my wife is still Janet Scott to anyone who knew her as a child. It's just something you have to know when you live on our village!

I started off doing my family tree a few years ago and now it has over 11,000 names in it mainly from our village and surrounding villages of Endon, Horton and Bagnall. It quickly became apparent that if your grandparents were born on the village then I'm related to you. One of the village characters, Harvey Durber used to greet people he didn't recognize with *"Oo at" "At a strug?"* (a strug is a lost pigeon which is applied to a stranger) Probably because they didn't understand him, they would say "I'm new on the village". His response would be something like, *"Theyt ad better watch ite, thee dustner know oo theyt towkin abite. Weyre ow kin dust know"*

Harvey was well known around the village and he certainly divided opinion. Some knew him as a man who treated his wife and family appallingly even by the standards of the times. Others saw him as a comic character walking around the village in his clogs carrying a huge log on his back. *"Luk wat arv funt."* *"Wee at gooin"* and *"Dust ere owd Judders Jed"* were phrases often used by him.

The older generation didn't have much time for him because *"Ey let ale git better onim"*. and *"Ey anner dun a tap since woower"* I have often heard this assertion that he was work shy rebuffed by *"Eh can if eh wants. Ar remember em shoveling fower fower month durin big snoo in fowerty seven. Imen Fred Werthy kept rude oopen"*, *"Non on us wud av any snappen if eet wunner fer im"*

However there was another side to him. He was, along with Jack Davenport the first person from the village to go to grammar school and when I broke my leg, one morning I woke to find my veg patch had been dug over by him when he was over 80 years old. *"The*

Afowereets Owgun

costner do it thee sell young Agan, if theyts brok thee leg". Agan was my dads nickname.

..

The D's & E's

Dade	Teaching baby to walk by supporting under arms	Old English *dade*
Deck	To stop *"Deck it wut"*	
Delf rags	Pit clothes	
Dinged	Bruised apple or car bodywork	Medieval English dingen
Dinnering	Official dinner	
Doffer	A bet type or dare challenge *"Arl doffer thee"*	
Donny	Childs hand *"Theytad better gitthesell sum gloves onthee donnies erelse thee fingersell drop off"*	
Drop on	To find something by chance. *"Eys dropped on theere, er looks a belter".*	
Drumble hole	Wooded valley between fields	
Ever likely	No wonder *"Theytell ever likely bey... at wom in*	

	this. Eets startvatin mon"	
Exings	Marriage bans	
Ext	To ask *"Ast extem"?*	

Pleen Iteseed

Doffering and leckering was a pastime that children especially used to take part in. It's generally a dare.

"Arl doffer thee to jump ower bruck"

"Bags Arl goo foggy" (I will go first)

"Bags Arl goo laggy" (I will go last)

"Arl goo seggy" (I will go second)

The position you chose depended upon how much you fancied the doffer or how impossible you thought it was for the others to do sometimes it was best to go last so that if everyone else failed you could demonstrate your abilities.

A lecker is simply a different name for the same thing.

The bruck mentioned above is the River Trent which winds its way through the village fields and was an ever changing playground for us damming it in the summer to create a swimming pool or to admire when it was in full spate in the winter.

One of the games we played, and often involved leckering, was pole vaulting over the brook. This was fine in the summer but in the winter if you got wet it was a long walk home!

Drumble holes are steep valleys cut out of the hillside that are fenced off to stop cattle from falling into the stream that is invariably at the bottom. They are so steep that in places grass doesn't grow on the sides and are always wooded, which make fantastic places for kids to explore.

These are places that give insight into what is underground as the stratigraphy is exposed. The sides are so steep no grass grows on them and you can disappear from view in an instant. On a couple you could see seams of coal. The streams are fed from springs higher up the hillside and never run dry and usually in certain spots the occasional trout hides away under the overhanging bankside. Such scars, cutting across the landscape are also barriers to wildlife trying to traverse the fields but are also highways for foxes and other predators seeking to move unnoticed in the landscape.

Childer pleed iteside ow dee. Mothers didn't want then in the house. After school mates came round and asked if you were "*coming ite*". This doesn't mean the same thing today! The only stipulation was that you had to be back when the lights came on. As I got older my dad said I had to be back before the last bus got in, which was 11.30. I was 18 at the time!

Of course we played *nogger* with a *casey* and jumpers as goal posts. Frantic affairs with teams as many as twenty a side if a game was on you would ask to "join in". Team selection was a brutal affair as you soon found out how people viewed you. Teams were picked in turn "*Arl av Cozza,*" "*Arl av Decker*" etc in turn until some lads were right at the back of the pecking order. Goalie was usually someone with a big pair of glasses or who couldn't run properly.

We would play on a pitch that was worn out clay, that dust rose off when the ball hit it. At half time if someone had any money or sometimes we would all put our money in to buy a bottle of pop which we would all have a swig from.

Sometimes the girls would come and watch. I don't know why but when that happened the intensity of the game seemed to increase!

Of course playing outside wasn't always as safe as I'm perhaps making it sound. Children often threw stones at other kids on the village and sometimes this caused "damage"

I know this is a bit extreme but my mum and her friend Betty Cope were machine gunned in the war whilst they were walking down a lane to Milton! A German bomber flew over and spotted them and opened fire. They both had to dive in a ditch and the corn fields around them caught fire. She told me that the plane was so low she could see the swastika on the side and the person machine gunning them!

That certainly didn't happen every day in fact Brown Edge saw little of the war, The closest action was a land mine that landed in a field on Biddulph Moor and rattled a few windows. However we did see an aircrash when a liberator Bomber crash landed in a field and caught fire. Florence Adderley (nee Simcock) said that she was playing in the field when it came down the first person out was a woman, who before she ran for cover as all the other crew did, she calmly took her comb out and combed her hair before hiding behind a wall!.

Of course all the lads of the village saw the plane coming down and went to investigate. My dad who was one of these lads told me that the plane was on fire and Sam Bratt, another village character, and a veteran of the first war, went inside the plane as it was on fire to get out the crew not realizing that they had already escaped. Dad said his hair caught fire. No one was impressed by the Americans who were hiding behind the wall.

The Police put a guard on the plane but most of the kids managed to get trophies with the Perspex and aluminum particularly prized.

Just about the only photograph I have with more than one of my Uncles on there! Uncle Gordon with his pipe in his mouth, Dad leaning against the decker and Uncle Edwin hiding between the two.

Afowereets Owgun

The F's

Facy	Cheeky child "*Eys rate (or reet) facey*"	
Fang	To catch hold of "*Arl fang otathee if ar seys thee doin it agen*"	Norse *fanga*
Farming	Used in a phrase such as: "*Wot at farming at*"? ie looking or doing	
Favour	To look like "*Eh favours is feyther*"	
Firk	To scratch or probe with a stick usually	OE fercian
Flirt	To throw especially with a stick	
Flit	Nobody moves house in these parts, they flit	ME flitten
Fob	To move forward in torrs or marbles	
Fodder road	Trough in front of cows	
Fogs, foggy	Claiming to go first "*Bags I goo foggy*"	
Fold	Little field	
Fother	Feeding beast	

Afowereets Owgun

Fotherbin	Grain store	
Franked	Late for work	
Fuffle	Fussing around	

A photograph taken in July 1892 of William Trebilcocks funeral to send to his family in Cornwall. Although the church is instantly recognisable it's worth noting that there were no houses built on School Bank at that time and there was a set of steps running past Church House.

Poaching

This is nothing to do with eggs!

Another pastime that the men on the village seemed to be preoccupied with was poaching. Even law abiding and God fearing men would take part in this activity. Somehow it was never accepted that anything wild could belong to a landowner. This was a long and established tradition which sounds like something from the days of Robin Hood, and had the same connotations. It was almost a badge of honour to be sent down for poaching.

I remember travelling around, and dad would say every now and then, *"Uncle Bill was in there for a while"*. I remember this included Shrewesbury and Knutsford gaol and several other places

There were several tactics employed and each poacher had his favourite. For rabbits, long nets, puss nets with ferrets, snares or hunting with lurchers were the options. The more skilled poachers could call hares out of a field, net partridge and know where and what day to catch lampreys out of the brook.

I remember Joe Bacca showing me how to make puss nets and how to catch hares with them. He said that hares were creatures of habit and if you made them lift and run they went round in a big circle until they came back to the same field if not the same spot. So if you watched where they went you could put a net in that spot (his favorite netting spot was a five barred gate) they would jump into the net.

Of course foraging for food was not illegal despite farmers constantly chasing you off the fields. Mushrooms, bilberries and blackberries were and are free to those who collect them, and certain fields had the best mushrooms. It was a close secret which fields were mushroom fields and this changed year after year. However fields with horses in were odds on as being the best.

Poaching was not the only illegal activity taking place in our village. Strange as it might seem to people nowadays who are bombarded daily by adverts for betting, bingo and lottery games all over the T.V. Off-course betting was illegal until 1960 and most of

Afowereets Owgun

the men used to bet on horses or cards before this time. Certain advantageous spots were the haunt of men meeting up for a bet. These spots had several escape routes and were so situated that the village bobby could be spotted from afar.

Again, another unknown Great, Great Grandfather. I suspect it is Francis Tomkinson

The G's

Gansey	Cardigan "*Theyt adbetter get thee gansee on erelse theytl bey getting chincough*"	
Gather	Fester "*Gitthesen some bread on that er else itl bey gatherin*"	OE gatherian
Gaumed-up	Covered in dirt "*Theyt ow gaumed up*"	
Gaup	Talking loudly	ME galpen
Ginnel	Narrow space between buildings I suspect that this is a word that comes from the Potteries.	
Gormers	Hay cart extensions	
Gosterer	Someone who boasts a lot. "*Eys a gosterer ey is*"	
Graunch	Grind teeth like sheep do "*Theyt Graunchin on em*"	
Grindlestun	Grind stone	ME grindel-stan

Afowereets Owgun

Grued-in	Ingrained dirt	
Hard-faced	Impudent	
Hare-shorn lip	Hare lip	
Hodge	Stomach	
Hullock, a great	Fat person	
Hullock, idle	Lazy person	
Hutched	Haunched *"Thets sittin o hutched up"*	
Hutched-up	Crowded together *"Hutch up apiece so as arcun sit dine"*	

The old Sandy Lane Chapel being demolished.

Feytin

There was always rivalry between villages and quite often this spilled over into a *feyt*. Sometimes this was organized and sometimes just happened, however people from neighbouring villages were always treated with suspicion. Our neighbour, that was really always seen as a rival was Endon or *Yen* as we called it. I don't know exactly why they were seen as being different but perhaps it was something to do with their men traditionally did not work down the pit. Anyway Yen sounds like hen so we called them *Yen muck* indeed there is a song we sang to them. It boasted that we had six church bells and they only had one. The song went something like this. "How does you gar-den grow" (a descending scale of six syllables) to which we gleefully shouted at them the answer, "Muck" (as they only had one bell in their church). From such simple things great merriment was achieved!

Fights between men were less common and if they were not pursued too far, were again tolerated. Sometimes a fight would lead to more terrible consequences. A fight between men who had just come out of the Holly Bush pub led to the unfortunate death of one man and another led to someone going home and getting a shotgun and killing his cousin. But when I was a lad fights in the playground were common almost a daily occurrence and was just the way of things. Indeed if they were "fair" fights they were almost encouraged and laughed off. Not to fight was seen by everyone as lacking moral fibre.

Our next door neighbor *Jack Denput* (Davenport) was the most kind and gentle man who along with Harvey Durber (already mentioned) were the first lads to pass their 11 plus test and go to Grammar School. Jack was a boxer in the Army and turned professional. I can remember hearing him punching a bag hung from the ceiling of his shed.

To harden him up he would swim across Knypersley pool breaking the ice if necessary! He wasn't a drinker apart from his home brew!

Afowereets Owgun

Feytin! Possibly outside the New Inn, Sandy Lane, Brown Edge. I know it's one of my Great Great Grandfathers but which one?

Notice the clogs on his feet.

The J & K's

Jack-sharp	Stickleback
Jib	To give in or to resist
Jinny spinner	Daddy long legs
Jowl	Hit on Head
Just now	Later on
Keggy	Left handed
Kedge	To steal or to borrow also as in to kedge a lift
Kiggle	Wobble on a chair
Keemers	Glasses or to peer over the top of glasses
Kecks	Trousers
Kim-kam	Gossiping ie kim-kamming. *"Dustner they go kim cammin behind mar back"*

Afowereets Owgun

The Pits

Although coal mining was probably the largest employer over the last two hundred years for our village, it would be wrong for people to think that this meant families were all poor and deprived. Some jobs were extremely well paid.

Before the Second World War, the mines were privately owned and most operated by employing buttey men or private foremen who paid their gang depending upon success. They were not employed by the mines. There was also a difference between a collier and a miner. A collier was a skilled occupation and regarded as such when it came to pay. My great grandfather on my mothers side, William Pepper, lived in Smallthorne and was a crutter which meant he opened up the drifts or faces so that the colliers or hewers could start to produce coal. This was a skilled job and required a good knowledge of geology. He went to work down the South Wales coalfields in the 1860's and made a fortune. So much in fact that he was supposed to have paid the wages of the men at Sneyd pit during the general strike. While he was in South Wales he bought a pub just so that he could have a drink on a Sunday!

Of course it was dangerous work for those who worked underground. All miners could be identified at a glance as they all wore a badge of office, that blue scar somewhere usually on their face or forearm that meant that they had been cut and coal dust had got in and left its tattoo for evermore.

Miners coughed up the filth and spat it out wherever they went and most people recognized this as acceptable except on the bus where there was always a sign forbidding it! Yet when they arrived up on the surface the first thing they wanted was a fag, usually a Woodbine or a pipe filled with twist!

Their day was split into three, consisting of days, noons and nights. These were the shifts set by the mines and this meant that men always had time to get things done. They were either in the garden or out foraging for wood, mushrooms, or other wild produce. I have even heard stories of men going after rooks and netting spuggies (sparrows) to bolster the family's nourishment. When you

Afowereets Owgun

think that most men used to walk to the pit about 2 miles from our village, walk underground again to the face, be expected to shovel 10 tons of coal and then walk back again, you wonder how they managed to go out to the pub afterwards.

The truth is though, they were not really welcome within their own home until the children were in bed, as the homes that they lived in were often too small for the large families that used to exist.

Just before he died Bill Snape told me that on Bank End (part of Brown Edge) there were two women (or families) that had 32 children between them. He also told me that he could remember the men coming back from the First War in a terrible condition. Some couldn't talk for years, just mumbling.

The old retired colliers used to sit on the wall in the centre of our village and talk of the old days. and of course our bus company attracted people into the garage who would come and talk about all sorts of things that had happened,

A typical conversation world go something like:

"Eh up Tunny" says visitor to my Uncle Alan ignoring the other three brothers sitting around the stove pot. But who would speak for each other.

"Adoo atorate waist bin, ar anner seyn thee fer a foutneet o mower".

"Arv bin eelin, nokin on deeths dower arl tell thee siree, meed awee, still coughin mey guts up siree, but arm mendin nar". Says visitor

Loud extended coughing finished off with a spit of phlegm into the stove pot from about 20 feet away

"Theyt qwees ad a good eem, pity the didstne plee darts fer the Bush" Says a brother.

"Anyrood dust eyer, ast erd ood Jarvs jed". Says the visitor.

"Ar agen"? "Ey wuz jed last weyk anow" Says a brother

"Ner eys reet jed nar, eys fell dine steers, arv bin in that ice an them steers ar reet steer arl tell thee, Theyt neyds a breyther afe wee up". Says visitor

Nar tell me Jud, ow cum theys beyn up steer there? The asner beyn timpin arind theer at? Says brother

"Mey timpin? Neer ar anner. The costner go seyin things lark that theytl get mey inter mischief with er indowers"! Says visitor

"Well it wunner bey fost tarm wud it"? Says brother

"Arm gooin if they costner bey proper." Says visitor

"Weya askin that's ow". Says brother

"Arl bet eyl be buried in is fost wives grave" Says another brother

"Ney if Eedies got owt do with it eh wunner. Erl avim brunt!" Says a brother

"Anyrood, arv erd its goon snoo" Says visitor

"Ner its tow cood it wunner snoo till it wearms up a bit". Says brother

"Well arm goin wom" Says visitor

"No cooin in on Eedie nar, dust ere" Says brother

"Oss off you lot ar onner cowin eer agin" Says visitor

Theyt wut. Says brother

And he did.

Notice how the brothers (my uncles) never spoke to each other just to the visitor. Indeed they rarely spoke directly about the things that mattered, like running a very successful business. Somehow, they didn't need to. And yet when they went on holiday they seemed to

Afowereets Owgun

seek each other out whether that was Cornwall, Blackpool or the south coast.

I know that other peoples family photographs are not that interesting but this one captures a moment in time and describes life in many ways. This photograph is the wedding 1916, of my Great Aunt Sarah and Samuel Leake taken outside her next door neighbours at The Rocks, Brown Edge. Samuel Turner Snr (man with pipe and cap) and his wife Mary Anne. My G Grandparents had already seen the impact of the war when their daughter Rose lost her first husband. Left in Wakefield with four children, Granny had to travel there to help het bring up the family. Two more sons were to die in the conflict Allen (in uniform at the back) and Edwin (right, back row)

The little girl on the right front (its blurred because she didn't stay still) is the daughter of Samuel Turner Jnr (flat capper no 2) and his wife Harriet (fifth from left back row) who was to die like her elder brother had already from a diphtheria epidemic later that year. It is said that this epidemic killed a third of Brown Edge children. The two boys at the centre front. both died, Colin from a motorcycle accident and Arthur from consumption. The lady at the extreme right looking away is Great Aunt Alice who lost an eye and won't look at the camera and the guy on the extreme left if you look closely has a wooden hand. He lost his hand down the pit. Luckily it was his left hand. The young man, Harry, (between Great Granny Turner and Samuel Junior) also lost the use of his arm down the pit. In times when there was no social security or health service, heath issues meant the difference between prosperity, survival and death.

The L & M's

Labe	Stir up mud	
Laggy	Last "*Bags ar goo laggy*"	
Lamp or lomp	Hit hard	
Lay-overs for meddlers	Stupid answer for a personal question you don't want to answer	
Leck	To water	OE leccan
Lecking can	Watering can	
Lickering	Who can jump the furthest or run the fastest	
Lozzuck (about)	Idle person	
Lug	Knot in hair	Scandinavian *Lugga*
Made away	To have a cold "*Arv bayn meed awe siree*"	
Mardy	Spoilt child	
Maunch	To make a mess of a job "*Theest meed a reet maunch agin*"	

Afowereets Owgun

Mending	Recovering from illness	
Mess off	Go away	
Midden or Mixen	Muckheap	ME Midding OE mixen
Monstink	Unpleasant child	
Moppet	Moth	
Mowed-up	Dirty cluttered	
Myther or mayther	Worry *"Dunner mayther theesell surry theytl bay arate"*	OE moither

The *Skoow*

A village ditty sung over 100 years ago by Brown Edge School children, as told to Dudley Frost by his father...

"Pancake day is a very happy day

If you don't give us a holiday

We will all run away.

Where shall we run to,

Down Sandy Lane"!

Children on our village were quite fortunate in that there was a school provided by the local pit owner in 1840 and operated by a church trust set up in his name. In fact he provided two schools, an infants and a junior school. Over the years the junior school had developed a reputation for being a model school with an innovative headmaster (Walter Jones) who sought to not only to give children an academic education but also an education in life.

In the 1900's to the 1930's it was the envy of Staffordshire and people from all over the country would visit to see what innovative ideas Mr Jones had introduced. Of course the children were well schooled, as it were. To show how intelligent and educated the children were the headmaster and sometimes his visitor would ask questions from the class, and almost all the children would raise their arm. Mr Jones would look round the room and pick someone and it would always be the right answer. A former pupil of the time Mr Bob Cumberlidge told me that visitors were amazed at first, the eagerness to answer the questions and secondly, how correct the answers were. Bob also told me that they had indeed been schooled well. Those that knew the answer raised their right hand and those who didn't raised their left! Those who didn't know their right from left didn't raise either!

The pride and joy of the school and the children was the school garden. Children were shown how to grow fruit and veg and provide flowers for the house.

Maths and other subjects were woven into the lessons, which appeared to fascinate the children. People tell me of how they grafted tomatoes onto potatoes showing they were of the same family. The importance of cleanliness was emphasised to prevent disease and how to feed the plants to get bumper crops.

Discipline was hard from the earliest times there was an infants school as well on the village so the big school took children from 7 to 12 or 13 depending on their level of education and from there they went straight to work.

On their first day at the big school they all had the cane! Both boys and girls, so that they all knew what it was like.

Sometimes the more academic of the children were taken on as teachers. One villager Mr Frost told me about his first day as a teacher. Of course he knew all of the children there, so on his first day he had to cane all 120 children including his three younger brothers!

My Uncle Alan told me that sometimes the fruit in the garden was very tempting especially the raspberries. One weekend he and a couple of friends raided it. On the Monday morning, the headmaster and school nurse were in assembly and Mr Jones announced he was surprised to see everyone, as he had treated the fruit trees with a pesticide that had terrible effects upon humans. He had done it on Saturday when no children were around because even the mist generated would probably prove fatal. The nurse however had the antidote and so he called upon those who had been in the garden over the weekend to come forward for treatment. After a little hesitation they owned up and immediately received six of the best. The rest of their class were also caned in case someone had not come forward!

My granddad noticed Uncle Alan had been caned and so he had another six. Granddad said "If your teacher sees it fit to cane you so do I". How times change.

Some children however, were immune from punishment it simply made no difference. It is said that my Uncle Edwin was thrashed everyday by my granddad with his belt until the day he went in the forces. Hard as nails. Even in the Air Force he was placed with the Canadians as he was always in trouble! When he was 77 he was still working in our garage, fell off a ladder and smashed his knee requiring an operation to fix it together. He was at work within the week.

We have converted the school into a village hall and during this work an old guy came in and told me about his days at the school. He was a Goodwin and used to live at Bank End Farm and said his dad always made him finish milking before going to school so he was always late and had dirty clogs for which he received the cane every day. One day the headmaster was so upset he lost his temper and hit him across the face with the cane drawing blood from his ear. Anyway at the end of the day the headmaster asked to see him and gave him half a crown because he knew he had overstepped what was acceptable. He said that he had never told anyone else what had happened that morning until he told me some seventy odd years later.

Another unknown ancestor. Although something in the back of my mind says this was Samuel Mountford my G.G. Grandfather. Just look at that wheelbarrow! All of these old guys have cracking beards.

Afowereets Owgun

The N & O's

Narky	Bad tempered	
Neb	Peak of cap	
Neck	To drink fast	
Nesh	Feeling the cold easily	
Nogger	The game of football	
Nous	Knowledge	
Nowt	Naughty boy *"Theyt just a nowt"*	
Nyarling	Whining *"Stop thee Nyarlin, theytl get thesell a sutter"*	
Oction	Place Used as in *"All over the oction"*	
Off-side	Unwell	
Oss off	Go away	

Afowereets Owgun

Soolin and Geyzin

I can just about remember been woken up by my dad to be shown a strange sight. Men dressed as women, some "Blacked up" and singing the words of a song I can only remember the first line or so,

"Soul, soul, soul a cake

I pray thee for a soul cake"

Also the lines

"Red stockings blue garters

My shoes are made of leather"

So what's Guizing? Guizing is from the old medieval word guise "to dress up" from which we now get disguise. Luckily a couple of old brownedgers who have now passed away, Roy Knight and Frank Simcock told me the whole story and put me right., Frank who wrote the following down for me and said he could remember singing the Guizing song to me when I was little!

Souling was done in the morning for an apple, pear, plum a cherry or even a slice of cake.

Soul a soul a soul cake,

Pray good missus a soul cake,

Give me an apple and I'll be gone,

One for Peter, two for Paul,

Three for them who made us all.

Put your hands in your pockets,

Pull out your bright keys,

Go down to the cellar,

Afowereets Owgun

> Bring up what you please,
> An apple a pear a plum or a cherry,
> Anything good that will make us all merry.

Guizing was done at night.

> I have a little money box under my arm,
> Penny or tuppence would do it no harm,
> Threepence or fourpence would do it some good,
> The best little money box made of wood.

> Red stockings blue garters,
> My shoes are laced with silver,
> A red rosette upon my chest,
> And a guinea gold ring on my finger.

> Hop hop hop to the butchers shop,
> I dare not stay any longer,
> For if I do my ma will say,
> I've been with the lads over yonder.

> Christmas is coming and the pigs are getting fat,
> Will you put a penny in the old man's hat,
> If you haven't got a penny a halfpenny will do,
> If you havne't got a halfpenny then God bless you.

> .

> We are two or three hearty lads all in one line,

We all come a guizing till this time next year,

Fantastic stuff all that!

Hearing the Hop Hop Hop verse reminded me that my mother used to sing that to me. I think it was a skipping song I can remember other bits of that also

I made you look, I made you stare
I made the barber cut your hair
He cut it long, he cut it short
He cut it with a knife and fork

Sam, Sam the dustbin man
Washed his face in a frying pan
Combed his hair with a donkey's tail
Scratched his belly with his big toe nail

You know last night and the night before
Three tom cats came knocking at the door
One had a fiddle, one had a drum
One had a pancake stuck to his bum

We also had mummers. The mummers were all dressed up and nobody was supposed to know or ask who this secret band were. A bit like Santa.

This was passed to me from someone many years ago and I'm sorry that I can't remember who, but it was taken from an old lady from up Lask Edge. She remembered the play being performed in local pubs primarily at Christmas time.

Afowereets Owgun

Characters

King George , The Prince of Paradise, Slasher, Bealzebub, The Doctor & The Little Devil Doubt.

Devil Doubt

Open this dower n let mey in,
Fur I am one bound to win.
Whether I rise or whether I fow
arl bey doin may duty to please thee ow.
A room, a room is what I desire,
Stir up this ere fire,

N mak a late,
For to see this jovial act by nate
I act by nate, n ar act by dee,
I mean to act this jovial act before I goo awee
If they dustne belave these words I see,
Step in King George and clear the wee.

King George (no local twang used for King George)

Here art I, King George
The Noble champion bold, of all the world,
With my bright buckled sword down my side
I won ten thousand pounds in Gold
Because I have fought the fiery dragon
And bought him to the slaughter
By these means I won the King of Egypts daughter

Slasher

Here am I Slasher,
Brave, bold, gallant slasher,
Slasher is my name,
The Turkish Moor, from Biddle Mower
A knight of fame
If I fought a fate with thee,
I fear thou art not able

For as I draw my glittering sword
I'm sure I'll thee disable.
King George
Disable, disable?
I'm not in thy power
If I draw my glittering sword
I'm sure I'll thee devour
Stand back Slasher, let no more be said
If I draw my glittering sword

I'm sure to break thy head

Slasher

How canst thou break mine yed

For my yed is meed of iron, my body of stale

My hands of fearsome knuckle boon

I'll challenge thee to a fayt

Slasher fights the King and falls

Devil Doubt
Cow in the prince
The Prince of Paradise
Here am I the prince, the prince of paradise

King George King George

What hast thou done

Thou has killed and slain mine only son, mine only heir

Look there he lies a blaydin theere.

Arl pee a thousand pind

Afowereets Owgun

A doctor to engage

Devil Doubt

A doctor a doctor?

What kind of doctor?

The Doctor

Mak wee, mak wee

Fur arm a doctor!

Devil Doubt

Since when, since when.

How becomest thou a doctor?

Doctor

From Italy, Sicily, Germany, France and Speen

Arv nar cum to cure diseases in owd England ageen.

King George

    What diseases can you cure

Doctor

Ow sewerts

King George

All sorts, all sorts?

what kind of ailment is that?

Doctor

It's the Itch, the twitch, the palsy and gout

The peen that's within and the peen withite

Arv cured a man with 15 devils in his sool

An cast 20 ite

Surely I can cure this power chap.

Here tak a little out of mar bottle

And let it run down thee throttle

If thou are not quite sleen

Then rise up to fate ageen

Slasher

Mee back—mee back

Doctor

What's amiss with thee back

Slasher

My back is wounded

My heart is confounded

To be struck out of seven senses into four score

Likewise I have never seen it befower

Beelzebub

Here am I old Beelzebub

Over my shoulder I carry my club

In my hand a dripping pan

I think myssell a jolly old mon

Put up these swords and spears to rest

As peace and quietness is the best

I've lived in houses, lands and cities

I've sung all the songs and the ditties

I've seen the men eating dumplings and poncakes

I've seen Bulls and piglets running up the strait

Old peter comes up with a turmit cart

and got struck on the crown

And made him shout termits all over the town.

Afowereets Owgun

Little Devil Doubt

Here am I Little Devil Dite
If you don't give me money I shall sweep all of you ite
Money I want and money I crave
If you don't give me money I'll sweep you to the grave
Now ladies and gents as you sit at your ease
Put your hand in your pocket
And give what you please
If you haven't got a copper a silver will do
Pull out your puss and give us a few.

The P's

Pather	Like a dog	
Piece	Sandwich	
Pigcote	Pigsty	
Pikel	Pitchfork	
Pither	Pottering about	
Pobs	Bread and milk	
Pouse	Rubbish food	FR pouse
Powk	Sty in the eye	OE pocc
Proke	To poke	
Proker	Poker	
Puddled	Soft in the head	
Puss-nets	Rabbit nets	
Puthery	Hot sultry weather	

Afowereets Owgun

Keytin

Keytin was another popular pastime for children. Being over 800 ft above sea level and overlooking the Cheshire plain we get a bit of wind and a trip to Highest Point or Marshes Hill and whenever I go up there "It's a top coat colder" as we say. Up there I am always reminded about *Keytin* that to us was good fun. A kite purchased from a shop although guaranteed to work well, was not really fair. Making the kite was what it was about. Split cane and brown paper was the best combination. And all shapes and sizes worked in different types and speed of wind. Some needed a constant steady flow of air to enable them to work and by adjusting the angle of string and the teelings (tailings) some would work in different conditions. *If thee kate goos up an darn teelins are too big, if it waggles its arse it neyds mower.* Lads would to try and build kits that were different is some way to everyone elses. The largest, the smallest, the highest flyer and the furthest being the most often talked about. Sometimes you would attach one then wait until the string was so far out it was hanging on the floor then attach another kite, and so on.

One of these was a kite built by Sam Bang (Willott). It was being flown off highest point and had such a long string it was right across the Hollow which is a valley in our village. Indeed it was well over our church when the string broke. Sam and Uncle Edwin finally caught up with it some 4 miles away over Burslem. I tell you this story that happened almost 100 years ago now and I can tell that Uncle Edwin had an immense pride for that kite which had become legendary in our village.

Sam Bang was a bit of a nowt as we say round here and I have already described Uncle Edwin to you! One of their tricks as boys was to put sods of earth onto peoples chimbleys (chimneys) and smoke them out of their houses!

Another favourite pastime for children was Dutch arrows! The idea here was to take a twig or stick out of a bush and carve a point at one end and spit the other end to insert some flights made from cardboard, binding them in with string. You then create a notch just under the flights and wind string round your hand and attach the other end to the arrow with a slip knot and then throw it. The best Dutch arrows could fly for considerable distances. Of course we would then have competitions to see how far we could fire them.

The best wood to use would be holly or privet. A cane was also useful but not completely acceptable!

Brown Edge is well blessed with clay and as lads we used this to good effect with canes of willow, pressing half a handful of clay on to the end and then flirting this at the opposing lads who had another clay mine! Occasionally if my memory does not deceive me we also used to flirt it at the women coming back from the shops. Good job we only had a village bobby and the idea there was to get him with snowballs!

We also had sprags, catties or twing fuds. A set of catapults made from holly was the best. After a while you didn't have to aim it just became instinctive. You just looked at where you wanted to hit and let loose.

Thinking back we all had knives, it's a wonder we survived.

The Q & R's

Queedle	See saw	
Quiggle	Rock on legs of chair or leaning back on the back 2 legs of a chair *"Dunner qweedle on back of that cheer"*. In our family this is also called kee wowing.	
Rammel	Mongrel dog. This was also used to describe a rough boy.	
Rathes	Hay cart extensions	
Rattle-chops	Talkative person	
Rawnged	Strained reaching up or carrying something	
Razzered (up)	Worn out	
Rift	Belch	Norse Rypta
Rindle	Small brook	
Rinkers	Marbles	
Risen-on	Feeling cold usually in a morning when leaving home	
Ronk	In a bad temper or simply a bad person	

Afowereets Owgun

Rumpty-fizzer	"Naughty but nice" person	

    Now here is someone I know, My Great Granny Turner (nee Twigge) with either my Dad or Uncle Allen on her knee. She passed away in 1928 aged 65. She looks ancient with her bonnet on.

    She was born in LLandegrii near Bethesda in Wales but her father Ralph Twigge, was from Butterton near Leek. Quite a few Butterton families including Mycocks & Salts moved there to work in the slate mines, when the copper mining ended in the 1850's. There are Butterton Twigges all over the world, still in mining in South Africa, Canada USA and Australia.

Of Pubs and Churches

Brown Edge had a reputation for being a little bit lawless and a cultural backwater. A bit like the Wild West you might say. My first day at work in Stoke, a colleague asked me where I was from and when I told him he said *"Oh dear, they still eat their babies up there!"* It wasn't quite as polite as that you understand.

I think that was also the view of many people, especially those in the clergy who felt that much work needed doing to save these Moorlanders. As I have previously said we had seven pubs, the Holly Bush, Rose and Crown, New Inn, Roebuck, Lump of Coal, Foaming Quart, Colliers Arms and of course the Working Mans Club. There was also rumored to be another long long ago called the Unhinging of Doors but who knows? This is for a village of 500 people at the beginning of the 20th century,

And people really knew how to drink! They even had drink at work. Grandad worked down Ford Green chainworks making anchor chains for liners including it is said, the Titanic. He was entitled to a quart of ale every break. He wasn't a particularly heavy drinker, but many others were. Every night as well, and twice on a Sunday. A man usually drank between six and 10 pints a night. Arthur Berry wrote a monologue called the Steady Six which described someone's moderation! Some heavy drinkers drank considerably more. It is said that Uncle Edwin held the record of 22 pints a session in the Lump of Coal, never to be beaten and only equalled by my cousin (his son).

As a result I have severe doubts about all this modern advice about drinking in moderation!.

There can be no doubt however, about the issue of smoking. I can honestly say that you could not see the other side of the Working Mens Club because of smoke, *"Thee cust cut it with a neef."* . It was horrific. All this drinking smoking and betting had a much worse effect though, it was a drain on family resources and caused the worst behaviour in many cases. As a result, people obviously felt much needed to be done. Whilst we had several meeting houses for Christian gatherings prior to the 19th century, we eventually have built up an incredible total of nine religious buildings consisting of six chapels one parish church and two missions from neighboring parishes. Just about the same number of pubs.

One of these chapels came about as a result of a Methodist evangelical preacher who came all the way from Cornwall and died after 3 weeks of preaching.

William John Trebilcock.

The following is an excerpt from the memorial Number of the Joyful News, a Cliff College publication, dated June 8th 1893, which has been confirmed by the Archivist of Cliff College on April 22nd 2009.

"A stranger to most of our workers, William John Trebilcock, a Cornishman, a strong, robust looking, sturdy young man, and when he was sent to work in Staffordshire, among the miners of Norton-in-the-Moors, his manly Christianity won from them respect and love. His ministry to the rough colliers was greatly blessed.

A revival broke out, and many of the most Godless turned from sin and became truly converted. Mr. Trebilcock spared no paths for their salvation and it was when putting forth extra effort to bring some of them to Christ that he caught the chill, which brought on rheumatic fever that laid him low.

A loving, weeping people bore him to his grave in the country churchyard on the Staffordshire hillside and his name will ever dear to many who will be his "Crown of rejoicing" in the day of the Lord.

He loved his work: no greater joy or honour would have he desired than to die as he had lived, preaching the glorious truths of the Gospel of Christ.

We have just heard that a new chapel is to be built at Norton-in-the -Moors and we believe it is largely owing to the devoted labours of Brother Trebilcock that such an even has become possible. (I understand this to be Sandy Lane Chapel).

We praise God for this good man's connection with us, and feel that it is no small honour to have his name among the list of the glorified saints of the "Joyful News" Mission.

Bro. Trebilcock departed this life on July 23rd 1892."

The Rev Page MA Vicar of Brown Edge wrote the following in 1915 "....The memory of Trebilcock is still green and his last resting place is cared for by loving hands. His visit to the village lasted three weeks, some days of which were spent in bed with pneumonia caused by sleeping in a damp bed ,ended his service here. People still speak of his open air meetings and of his fearless crusade in the public houses, where, accompanied by his melodeon, he sang his songs of deliverance and knelt to pray, too often amidst the jeers of those seated there. But he lived long enough to do some reaping, for ten men changed their lives owing to his faithful words. He speaks still and like John Wesley from a village tombstone, reminding us we are here to reap and gather the eternal fruit, pointing men to the mansions on high.

Another Chapel was Hugh Bourne's Chapel, the founder of the Primitive Methodists. Although everyone knows Primitive Methodism started after an open air meeting at Mow Cop, in fact it was originally planned to be on Marshes Hill, Brown Edge (Brown Edge was part of Norton Parish in those days) but bad weather forced it to be cancelled. An additional complication was that Hugh was still a churchwarden at Norton Church and this meeting would have compromised him and the Rector of Norton Church somewhat if it was held in their parish. Marshes Hill adjoined what became his Chapel, and are now called Chapel Cottages but is in Endon Parish. Hugh never intended to leave the Church of England and I have been told that his brother remained as churchwarden after Hugh was forced to leave.

We now have two pubs one of which is facing demolition and the other recently upgraded by a village resident who does not use the pub for sole income.

We have a Parish church that no longer has a Vicar and its vicarage sold off. The two remaining chapels are only used by a handful of people. How times change.

It is difficult to explain the scale of social impact of the Churches and Chapels here on Brown Edge. Probably one of the biggest days was the anniversary walk around the village of the various Sunday Schools that took part and the children got dressed up in their best finery. Somewhere in my mind I can remember my sister wearing an Easter bonnet!

Sunday School started for me at the Chapel when I was a lad. No on reflection it started way before that. Older children used to "call" for me in my pram and take me to Sunday. There wasn't any option really. Mr Albert Mountford was the principal driver of the Sandy Lane Chapel Sunday School. It originally was held in the old Working Mans Club hut and then grew to having its own purpose built premises. You had an attendance record book made out of some kind of linen paper as you could peel the strings out of it.

There were around 200 children in that Sunday School and then there was the church and other chapels also. We must have been a God fearing community.

The Chapel Sunday School outing. Gordon Turner with the cap on and Albert Mountford next to him. Just look how many busses we used to take!

The S's

Scen	To squint	
Scrat	Scratch like a hen	ME scratten
Scrawl	Crawl	
Scrawm	Mean person getting money together	
Scrawp	Scratch or damage	
Scrit	Weak one in the litter	
Scuft	Slap	
Seg	Calous on skin	
Seggy	To claim second place	
Senna-tucked	Stiff after sitting down	
Set	To rent out	
Settle	A comfortable armchair	OE setel
Shape for	Preparing to	
Sheed	Spill a lovely word so much more descriptive "*Lukite theet sheydin it*"	
Shippen	Cow shed	

Shotties	Marbles
Side	Clear away (a table) as in, to put the plates on the side
Sken	Squint
Slat	Throw down
Slither pudding	Slipshod work
Slopstone	Sink
Snapping	Food
Snapping time	Dinner time (lunch)
Snead,	Scythe
Sneap	To snub
Snide away	Overrun with vermin
Snotty	Bad tempered
Soakies	Bread and milk
Sprags	Catapults.
Steer	Steep *"Just look at that roof its steer"* Or confusingly *"Them steers are reet steer"*

Old Soldiers

In these centenary years of the Great War we remember those villagers who fought for their country from our village. The majority of these men were in reserved occupations and had no need to fight but most did so. The first war was a turning point in peoples understanding of what war was. The men who returned were never the same again.

My Great Uncle Bill Tomkinson joined up in 1914 and joined the North Staffs 1/5th Battalion along with many other Brown Edgers. His lungs were full of coal dust and then he was gassed as well! He did make it home despite fighting at Hohenzollern Redoubt where they went over the top kicking a football shouting *"Up the Potters"*. I can just about remember him. Before I was born he lived in our house with my grandmother and grandad. He slept in the bed in the day and they at night. He only received half the war pension because he was shot in the back and he refused to have the bullet removed because he was told it was unlikely he would walk again. He refused treatment and it cost him his pension.

Of those that went into war twenty six didn't come back including my two other Great Uncles Edwin and Allan Turner. Two others did come back Hiram Houldcroft and Joseph Kennet Goodwin but they died shortly after from war wounds. Joseph Goodwins memorial plaque was found recently in a junk shop in California and has kindly been sent back to us by a thoughtful person.

These plaques were presented to the families of all those lost in the war.

When we were converting the old church school to our Village Hall (some 30 years ago), we found two memorial tablets with the names of the old school boys that died in the First War. I subsequently found that these had been the cause of a post war contretemps between the school headmaster and the Vicar. There was already a memorial in the church and the vicar didn't want another. The headmaster lost his job over the subsequent argument.

So some 70 years after this incident we erected a memorial outside the Village Hall along with another tablet to those who had died in the Second World War. There is one error. We had two Hancock brothers who were guardsmen (actually they were both pallbearers at King George 5th funeral) who both died on the same day at Dunkirk defending the retreat.

Unfortunately there was another Brownedger with the same name who died. The people who put the list together of Brownedgers, were aware of all 3 of the people who died but how one was missed off I don't know. It might have been the mason who carved the tablet thinking there was a duplication. Anyway, we didn't notice until it was too late.

All the families of the men who were killed in the Great War had a plaque presented to them.

Twenty eight were produced and we currently know of the existence of four.

The T's

Ted	To turn over hay
Thrape	To thrash *"Dunner thrape at it lad, tak it easy"*
Thunge	Bumping around
Timber-toed	Pidgeon toed
Timping	Hanging around. Catching the eye of the ladies.
Tit	Horse. This caused much merriment when I went to Grammar School. It took me a while to understand just what they were laughing at. Horse racing was always called *"Tit mucking"*.
Tittle-stomached	Squeemish
Trappings	Bits and pieces. *"Thee cust pack thee bags n trappings an gitthee gun nar"* Gordon Turner sacking someone!
Tow-rag	Oatcake or naughty boy
Tucks	Lots of it!
Tun-dish	Funnell
Turmit	Turnip
Tweedle	See saw

Dogs & Pigeons

"It's a wake mon as nayds a big dog". Is a saying on our village so terriers and staffies were the order of the day. There were a few exceptions: Lurchers. These were not entirely greyhounds but were crosses with something else specifically designed to catch rabbits.

Dogs were everywhere on Brown Edge, very often they were let out and roamed the streets. Occasionally someone would catch a rat in a trap and then would take it down the playing fields and let it go for their dog to chase. No need for a television then in Brown Edge!

There used to be a white bulldog that got onto our bus and sat under the stairs and went to Hanley on its own (7 miles) get off, go to a butchers, catch the bus again and come home with a bone in its mouth! Another, from the Holly Bush Pub, would raid Garners shop for food and I have seen him running up the street with a string of sausages in his mouth.

However the strangest thing was one day my daughter Victoria, who was under two and had not yet mastered the English language properly said "Look a dog with a pig in its mouth"! We didn't believe her and thought she was making it up. About 10 minutes later she said the same thing. So looking out of the window I couldn't see anything amiss so I asked her to take me to where it had come from and she led me to the farm and sure enough the dog had got into a farrowing pen and taken two piglets!

I suppose it has to be pointed out that there is only one working farm on the village now and only two in the whole parish. Whereas some 50 years ago there were at least fifteen substantial farms and innumerable smallholdings. In a morning in the summer the Proctor brothers who farmed Bank End Farm used to let the cows walk out into the road on their own one at a time when they had finished milking. They used to find their way down a road across a main road junction through a housing estate and into their field. At least half a mile away.

It was not unusual to see farmers walking the bull round the village to visit other farms. We are not an agricultural village any more.

Even the pigeons have gone! At one time, there must have been twenty pigeon cotes in our village and now there are two that I know of. Pigeon racing was simply part of the culture. If you didn't have a cote yourself (they aren't lofts up here) then you would often be "attached" to one, sometimes helping out, sometimes sitting waiting for them to come home on a Saturday with your mates with a can of corn that you would rattle if the bird was close, *"Cummon, common"* was shouted out and you would keep still, least you scared the bird off.

If you had a car you would go training and loose the pigeons from their wicker basket at a progressively further distance from home. Some owners had their own tricks. Having a loft low down the valley was a help as it meant those pigeons further on would be attracted to go down and then climb up whereas others said being on top of the hill was an advantage because the cote could be seen easier. I know of one who treated his birds to a drop of sherry!

Most of the pigeon men were miners or ex miners all dressed the same cloth cap, collarless shirt, muffler round their neck, jacket and corduroy trousers. A few were farmers however and professional people like Howard Cornes, a local well to do builder.

The Rest

Unscrewgle	To open eyes
Up-bonk	Uphill
Waft	Strength or endurance *"Eys got sum waft ey as"*
Wag, to play	Bob off school
Werrit	Worry *"Dunner werrit thesel"*
Without	Unless
Wog	Steal
Wom	*"R ice"* Home
Woppit	Wasp
Yawp	Loud mouthed *"What at yawpin at"*
Yorks	String tied below knee on trousers
Yowther	Youth *"Nar stedy thesel yowther they dustne neyd getting theysellinter myther"*.

Famous Sons (or daughters)

Well this is an easy one. We don't have any! Possibly the most famous person or event was when Stanley Matthews crashed his car on the bend coming in to the village which is often now called Stanley Mathews corner! We of course had lots of characters, famous in their own village. My Uncle Gordon always said, and several others have repeated this, that the man who invented cats eyes lived in a house on Willfield Lane but having watched a programme about Percy Shaw on the TV, it seems very unlikely.

So some people reading this might say you have forgotten about David Steele the England Cricketer who won the BBC Sports Personality of the Year. I haven't forgotten him, he was indeed a hero to me and I can still remember his dad listening to him score a century for England on one of our buses that was parked outside. But you see in this Village living here is fine but to qualify as a Brownedger you have to be born here. David was born at Bradeley a mile or so away and came to the village when he was a baby! If you think this is stupid (and it is) then for the Queens Silver Jubilee (1977) I remember a discussion going something like this at our Parish Council meeting

"Dust ere, wey givawee a medal fer owdest mon an woman fer last Qweyns Jewbilee (Victoria) *an granny Kneet lit bonfeer."*

So a discussion took place of who the oldest man on the village was for the forthcoming Silver Jubilee.

"Owd mon Siglee eys thoodest" "Ar eys neenty fower"

"Ner ey wonner bowen on village eys mother ad im dine yen"

Needless to say the younger members of the Parish Council and the press who were in attendance thought it better just to keep out of this one. No decision was made and medals were awarded!

Having said that we are extremely proud of David and his brother John for their cricketing exploits, however there is always one or two people who say, *"Ey was a better footbower thee knowst"* and do you know, he possibly was.

If I was asked to describe Brown Edge I would say there is one guy who described it better than anyone and that is Arthur Berry, often described as the Potteries Lowry. This in reality does Arthur a disservice in that his work has a much wider scope, including plays, monologues, poetry as well as his evocative artwork. Although he is claimed by the *"Potherbs"* as one of theirs, in reality he is a Moorlander at heart, as he himself says in his autobiography, A Three and Sevenpence Halfpenny Man.

"The village of Smallthorne is the last knuckle of the Pennine chain, the last little lump of a hill before the land becomes flatter and the Midlands begin. It is most definitely a part of the North, a part of the Staffordshire Moorlands, and whenever I go through this country I know it is my own clod, the place my tribe comes from. It is a world of stone walls and thin-soiled fields, where flat-capped, mufflered, peasant colliers own one-egg farms and stuff their money in the mattress. It is a place of feud and litigation where men know every stone in their own walls. They are a hard, independent people who know all their own tribe but don't necessarily trust them. They watch the cars and buses pass, spit, and say nothing. They are a stoical people who have one foot in the town and one foot in the country. They have been to the pictures and the billiard halls and also sold pigs at the cattle market. Their wives have usually a lot more to say and say it mostly to their married daughters who never live far away from their mams.

In these moorland places, families were often ingrown and all branches of the family known by different nicknames. Most of the men were known by nicknames as well —Styfe, Maunch, Cliggs, Spanner, Tittybottle, Workbag, Physic, Razor, Bottle, Jarve, were a few of the nicknames these men went by. From Nettlebank to Smallthorne, from Brown Edge to Ball Green, from Biddulph to Biddulph Moor, the distance between these pit village is no more than a mile or so and nowhere are you out of sight of the headsticks of a pit. It is a place of nettlebeds and pig stys, where tin roofed sheds house gleaming motorbikes, where every field is surrounded by a stone wall. This is the country of my heart. Both sides of my family originated from Brown Edge, a village no more than a mile and a half from the crowded streets of Smallthorne. Both my mother's father and my father's grandfather had been boys together in the same class in the church school there, and when they left school at ten years of age, they both went to work down the pit at Chatterley Whitfield Colliery, a mile away. This pit at that time was known as the Queen of the North Staffordshire coalfield and employed thousands of colliers. Mr Enoch Tomkinson, my mother's father, was known as Nocky and I shall begin my story with him. ..."

That describes the Brown Edge of my childhood almost as good as his paintings do! If you have never taken the time to look at his paintings then please do as they exude the souls of people and a way of life now gone.

Arthurs references to Brown Edge do not stop with his autobiography but are inserted in many of his works. For example the chipper in "A Little Goldmine" was found in a chip shop burnt down in Brown Edge which is based upon fact in that we did have a chip shop that was burnt down opposite the Lump of Coal which incidentally, is also mentioned in his book Dandelions.

If the *"Potherbs"* have put a claim on him, then we will be delighted for him to have a claim on us!

As they say around here, *Arl sithee siree.*